# Cinderella

Retold by Jenny Giles

Illustrated by Margaret Power

NELSON PRICE MILBURN

Once upon a time, there was a rich man
who had a beautiful daughter called Ella.
His wife had died a long time ago,
and he had married again.

His second wife was unkind to Ella.
She made her work hard all day long,
and Ella's clothes became ragged and torn.
When evening came,
Ella was always very tired.
She would sit down by the fire
in the ashes and cinders
to rest and keep warm.

2

The wife had brought
her two ugly daughters with her.
They were both as unkind as their mother.
"Look at you, down there
in the dirty ashes," they would say.
"We are going to call you Cinder-Ella,
because you are always sitting
in the cinders."

Cinderella felt very sad and lonely.

Then one day, a special invitation arrived,
saying that the King was going to hold
a Grand Ball at the palace.

Cinderella's stepmother and
the two ugly sisters were very excited.
"You can make new dresses for all of us,"
one of them said to Cinderella.
"We must have the most beautiful clothes
to wear to the ball."

"The King's son will be there,"
said the other sister, "and I have heard
that he is looking for a wife.
He might choose me!"

4

5

On the night of the Grand Ball,
Cinderella helped her stepmother
and her ugly sisters to get dressed
in their new gowns.

Then she watched them driving away.

As Cinderella went over to sit by the fire, tears began to roll down her cheeks.
"Oh, how I wish I could go to the ball," she said.

Suddenly, a kindly old woman
appeared beside Cinderella.
"I am your Fairy Godmother," she said,
"and I can help you go to the ball.
Follow me."

She went out into the garden,
and tapped an enormous pumpkin
with her magic wand.
Immediately, it turned into a fine coach!

Then six grey mice from the mouse trap
became six grey horses to pull the coach.

An old rat became the coachman.

"There!" said the Fairy Godmother.
"Now you can go to the ball, Cinderella!"

"But I cannot go to the ball
in these ragged clothes!" cried Cinderella.

The Fairy Godmother touched Cinderella
with her magic wand.
"Look!" she said. "You are now wearing
the loveliest gown in the land."

Cinderella was delighted.
She watched as her old slippers
changed into the most beautiful glass shoes
she had ever seen.

"Oh, thank you! Thank you,
Fairy Godmother," she cried.

"You can be on your way now, my child,"
said her Fairy Godmother.

"But there is one thing to remember!
You must leave the ball by midnight,
because then the magic will end,
and your clothes will be rags again."

"I will not forget," said Cinderella,
as she climbed into her coach.

When Cinderella walked into the castle
ballroom, everyone turned to look at her.
The Prince came towards her,
amazed by her beauty.
As the music began to play,
he took her hand.
Then he danced with her all night.

The ugly sisters sat beside their mother and said, "Who is that beautiful girl? We have never seen her before."

Everyone at the ball wanted to know who she was.

Cinderella was having such a wonderful time
that she forgot to look at the clock.
All too soon, the chimes of midnight
began to ring out.
"I must go!" she gasped to the Prince.
She ran out of the ballroom
and down the palace steps.
One of her glass shoes came off,
but Cinderella could not stop.

The Prince called to her,
but by the time he reached the doorway,
she had gone.

The Prince walked slowly down the steps.
He picked up the dainty glass shoe
and smiled to himself.
"Tomorrow I will get my servants to take
this shoe to every house in the land,"
he said.
"Whoever it fits will become my wife."

So the very next day,
the Prince's servants went from house
to house with the glass shoe.
Every woman in the land
tried to put it on.

At last, the servants arrived at
Cinderella's house.
The ugly sisters ran to meet them.
"Let me try the shoe!" cried one sister.
"It will fit me."

"No! Give it here!" cried the other.
"It is my shoe!"

The ugly sisters fought over the shoe.
They tried to squeeze their feet into it,
and so did their mother.

But it did not fit any of them.

17

Then the servants looked at Cinderella and said, "Every woman in the land must try this shoe."

The ugly sisters started to laugh. "But that is only Cinderella," they said. "She is too poor to wear such a fine shoe!"

One of the servants knelt down in front of Cinderella.  He held out the shoe and she slipped her foot into it.

It fitted perfectly!

Suddenly, Cinderella's Fairy Godmother appeared again.
She waved her wand, and once more Cinderella was wearing her beautiful ballgown and both glass shoes.

"So it was Cinderella at the ball!"
cried the ugly sisters.

"**She** was the beautiful girl
who danced all night with the Prince!"
cried their mother.

19

The servants took Cinderella
back to the palace
where the Prince was waiting.
He was delighted to see her again.
"Will you marry me," he asked,
"and become my wife?"

"Oh, yes," smiled Cinderella.

And so Cinderella and the Prince were
married, and they lived happily ever after.

# A play

# Cinderella

## People in the play

 Reader

 First Ugly Sister

 Cinderella

 Second Ugly Sister

 Stepmother

 Prince

 Fairy Godmother

 First Servant

 Second Servant

**Reader**

Once upon a time, there was a rich man
who had a beautiful daughter called Ella.
His wife had died long ago,
and he had married again.
His second wife was unkind to Ella.
She made her work hard all day long,
and Ella's clothes became ragged and torn.
The stepmother had brought her two ugly
daughters with her.
They were both as unkind as their mother.

**Stepmother**

Go and make the beds, Ella.
Then do the washing and scrub the floors.

**Reader**

When evening came, Ella was always tired.
She would sit down by the fire
in the ashes and cinders
to rest and keep warm.

**First Ugly Sister**

Look at you, down there in the dirty ashes.

**Second Ugly Sister**

We are going to call you Cinder-Ella,
because you are always sitting
in the cinders.

**Cinderella**

Oh, why are they unkind to me?
I am so sad and lonely.

**Reader**

Then one day, a special invitation arrived
for Cinderella's stepmother
and the two ugly sisters.
They were very excited.

**Stepmother**

Look! The King is going to hold
a Grand Ball at the palace!

**First Ugly Sister (to Cinderella)**

You can make new dresses for all of us.
We must have the most beautiful clothes
to wear to the ball.

**Second Ugly Sister**

The King's son will be there.
I hear that he is looking for a wife.
He might choose me!

**Reader**

On the night of the Grand Ball,
Cinderella helped her stepmother
and her ugly sisters to get dressed
in their new gowns.
Then she watched them driving away.

**Cinderella (crying by the fire)**

Oh, how I wish I could go to the ball.

**Fairy Godmother (appearing)**

I am your Fairy Godmother,
and I can help you go to the ball.
Follow me.

**Reader**

Cinderella followed her Fairy Godmother
into the garden.

**Fairy Godmother (tapping with wand)**

I will turn this pumpkin into a coach!
I will turn these six grey mice
into six grey horses to pull the coach.
And a rat will become your coachman.
Now you can go to the ball, Cinderella!

**Cinderella**

But I cannot go to the ball
in these ragged clothes!

**Fairy Godmother (tapping with wand)**

Look!  You are now wearing
the loveliest gown in all the land.

**Cinderella**

And I have beautiful glass shoes, too!
Oh, thank you, Fairy Godmother.

**Fairy Godmother**

You can be on your way now, my child.
But there is one thing to remember!
You must leave the ball by midnight,
because then the magic will end,
and your clothes will be rags again.

**Cinderella**

I will not forget.  Goodbye!

**Reader**

Cinderella walked into the ballroom,
and everyone turned to look at her.
The Prince danced with her all night.

**First Ugly Sister**

Who is that beautiful girl?

**Second Ugly Sister**

We have never seen her before.

**Reader**

Everyone wanted to know who she was.
Cinderella was having such a wonderful time
that she forgot to look at the clock.
The chimes of midnight began to ring out.

**Cinderella**

It is midnight!  I must go!

**Reader**

Cinderella ran out of the ballroom and down the palace steps. One of her glass shoes came off, but she could not stop.

**Prince (picking up the shoe)**

Come back! Come back!
Oh, no! She has gone!
I will get my servants to take this shoe
to every house in the land tomorrow.
Whoever it fits will become my wife.

**Reader**

The next day, the Prince's servants went
from house to house with the glass shoe.
Every woman in the land tried it on.
At last, the servants arrived
at Cinderella's house.
The ugly sisters ran to meet them.

**First Ugly Sister**

Let me try the shoe!  It will fit me.

**Second Ugly Sister**

No!  Give it here!  It is my shoe!

**Stepmother**

Stop fighting over that shoe.
I will try it.
Oh, no!  It will not fit me, either.

**First Servant (looking at Cinderella)**

Every woman in the land must try this shoe.

**First Ugly Sister (laughing)**

But that is only Cinderella.

**Second Ugly Sister**

She can't wear such a fine shoe!

**Second Servant (kneeling down)**

Let me see if this shoe will fit you.

**Reader**

Cinderella slipped her foot into the shoe.

**Cinderella**

It fits me because it is **my** shoe.

**Reader**

Suddenly, Cinderella's Fairy Godmother appeared again. She waved her wand, and once more Cinderella was wearing her beautiful gown and both glass shoes.

**Ugly Sisters (together)**

So it was Cinderella at the ball!

**Stepmother**

**She** was the beautiful girl who danced all night with the Prince!

**First Servant**

Come to the palace with us, Cinderella.

**Second Servant**

The Prince will be waiting for you.

**Reader**

Cinderella went back to the palace
with the servants.
The Prince was delighted to see her again.

**Prince**

Will you marry me, and become my wife?

**Cinderella (smiling at the Prince)**

Oh, yes.   I will marry you.

**Reader**

And so Cinderella and the Prince
were married,
and they lived happily ever after.

# I can make a
# Rhyme

Selected by Viv Lambert, illustrated by Richard Johnson

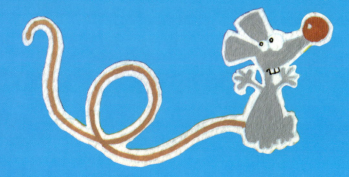

How to use this book...

1) Say the rhymes aloud, looking at the pictures for help

2) Look at the highlighted words and say them on their own

3) Find the sticker that rhymes with each highlighted word and put it in the right place

Ladybird

Humpty Dumpty sat on a **wall.**

Humpty Dumpty had a great **fall.**

All the King's horses

and all the King's **men**

Couldn't put Humpty together **again.**

Pussycat, pussycat, where have you **been?**

I've been to London

to visit the **Queen.**

Pussycat, pussycat, what did you do **there?**

I frightened a little mouse

under her **chair.**

One, **two**, buckle my shoe.

Three, **four**, knock at the door.

Five, **six**, pick up **sticks.**

Seven, **eight**, lay them **straight.**

Nine, **ten**, a big fat **hen.**

**fiddle,**

**spoon.**

**spout.**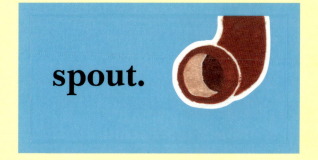

**rain,**

**cry.**

**ran away.**

**star,**

**sky.**

Hey, diddle, **diddle,**

The cat and the ⬚

The cow jumped over the **moon.**

The little dog laughed to see such fun,

And the dish ran

away with the ⬚

Incy Wincy Spider climbed

up the water

Down came the rain and

washed the spider **out.**

Out came the sunshine and

dried up all the

So Incy Wincy Spider climbed

up the spout **again.**

Georgie Porgie, pudding and **pie,**

Kissed the girls and

made them

When the boys came out to **play,**

Georgie Porgie

Twinkle, twinkle, little ⌐ ¬

How I wonder what you **are.**

Up above the world so **high,**

Like a diamond in the ⌐ ¬

Twinkle, twinkle, little **star,**

How I wonder what you **are.**